Fiery Kilauea volcano eruption, Big Island of Hawaii

Papillon's Hawaii

Featuring photography
by Mike Sedam

ALBION
PUBLISHING GROUP

Albion Publishing Group
924 Anacapa Street, Suite 4E
Santa Barbara, CA 93101

Project Managers:
Teresa Roupe and Angela Tripp

Contributing Editor:
Nicky Leach

Production Manager:
Joanne Station

Designer:
Linda Trujillo

Design Assistant:
Britta Bonette

Typesetting:
Graphic Traffic

Library of Congress Catalog Number: 91-76597
ISBN 1-880352-13-3

Special thanks to the
outstanding pilots and other employees at
Papillon Hawaiian Helicopters whose support
and assistance made this book possible.

PHOTOGRAPHS

Bob Abraham/Photo Resource Hawaii: 50 middle and bottom right, 51 bottom left. Rita Ariyoshi: 9 third from top, 13 bottom, 14, 17, 77 bottom, 82 middle, 89 top and bottom, 90 bottom right, 93 bottom. Bishop Museum: 12 top left and right, 12 middle and bottom left, 13 top, 57 top, 69 bottom. Randy Coon/Trilogy Excursions: 9 second from bottom. Damien Museum: 70-71 bottom inset, J.D. Griggs/U.S. Geological Survey: 10-11. C. Heliker/U.S. Geological Survey: 110 bottom. Herb Kane: 9 top, 57 bottom (collection of Nick G. Maggos). National Park Service: 121. Pacific Whale Foundation: 86-87, 87. Raz Rasmussen: 115 top and bottom, 115 middle right. Franco Salmoiraghi: 2-3, 116-117. Mike Sedam: cover, front flap top, inside front cover and page 1, 4-5, 6, 7, 8, 9 second from top and third from bottom, 11, 13 middle, 15, 16, 18-19, 20-21, 22, 23 top and bottom, 24 inset, 24-25, 26-27, 27, 28, 28-29, 29, 30-31, 31, 31 inset, 32-33, 34-35, 36-37, 37, 38-39, 40-41, 42-43, 44, 44-45, 45, 46, 46 inset, 47 middle and bottom right, 47 middle and bottom left, 48 top left and right, 48-49, 49 top left, 50-51, 51 middle left, 51 bottom right; 52-53, 54 inset, 54-55, 56, 58 bottom left and right inset, 58-59, 59 bottom, 60, 61, 62-63, 64-65, 66-67, 68, 69 top, 70 bottom inset, 70-71, 70-71 bottom inset, 71 top and bottom, 72, 73, 74, 74-75, 76-77, 77 top, 78-79, 80-81, 82 left and right, 82-83, 83, 84, 84-85, 85 bottom, 88, 88-89, 90 top, 90 middle and bottom left, 91, 92-93, 93 top, 93 middle inset, 94, 95, 96, 96-97, 97 right, 98-99, 99 top and bottom, 100 top and bottom, 101, 102-103, 106-107, 108, 108-109, 109, 110-111, 111 bottom, 112-113, 114-115, 115 middle left, 118-119, 119 top, 119 inset, 120 inset, 120-121, 122-123, 124-125, 125 top and bottom, 126, 126 inset, 127 top and bottom, 128 bottom left, 128 top and bottom right, inside back cover and back flap, outside back flap, back cover. Allan Seiden/Creative Focus: front flap bottom, 39 top right, 67 top right. T.J. Takahashi/U.S. Geological Survey: 104-105. G. Ulrich/U.S. Geological Survey: 9 bottom.

ILLUSTRATIONS

Linda Trujillo: 17, 20, 42, 64, 80, 106.

Sunset cruise off Honolulu, Oahu.

Wailau Coast, Molokai.

FOREWORD

Papillon Helicopters' mission brings excitement and satisfaction to myself and all the employees of Papillon. Our mission is to share an unparalleled experience of sight and sound. An experience that will create a memory forever of the untouched hidden side of Hawaii. A view of what the first natives saw when they reached the beautiful shores of the Hawaiian Islands.

To each of our customers their tour is a very special lifetime experience. To many it is tantamount to a spiritual experience, to others it is simply breathtaking and awesome, to all it is an experience of a lifetime for which virtually every customer is grateful.

Every year Papillon, with its sizable fleet of aircraft, flies the equivalent of 30 years of single pilot flying. From this broad base of exposure we have selected from our library of over 15,000 photographs some of the most classic images of the Hawaiian Islands. It is our pleasure to be able to share these with you so that you may continue to enjoy the experiences you have had on a Papillon flight. If you are a visitor to Hawaii who has not flown, you can, by means of this publication, get a glimpse of some of the incredible scenery found in the Eden called Hawaii.

Elling Halvorson

Elling Halvorson
President

Secluded beach near Pukoo, Molokai.

■ Contents

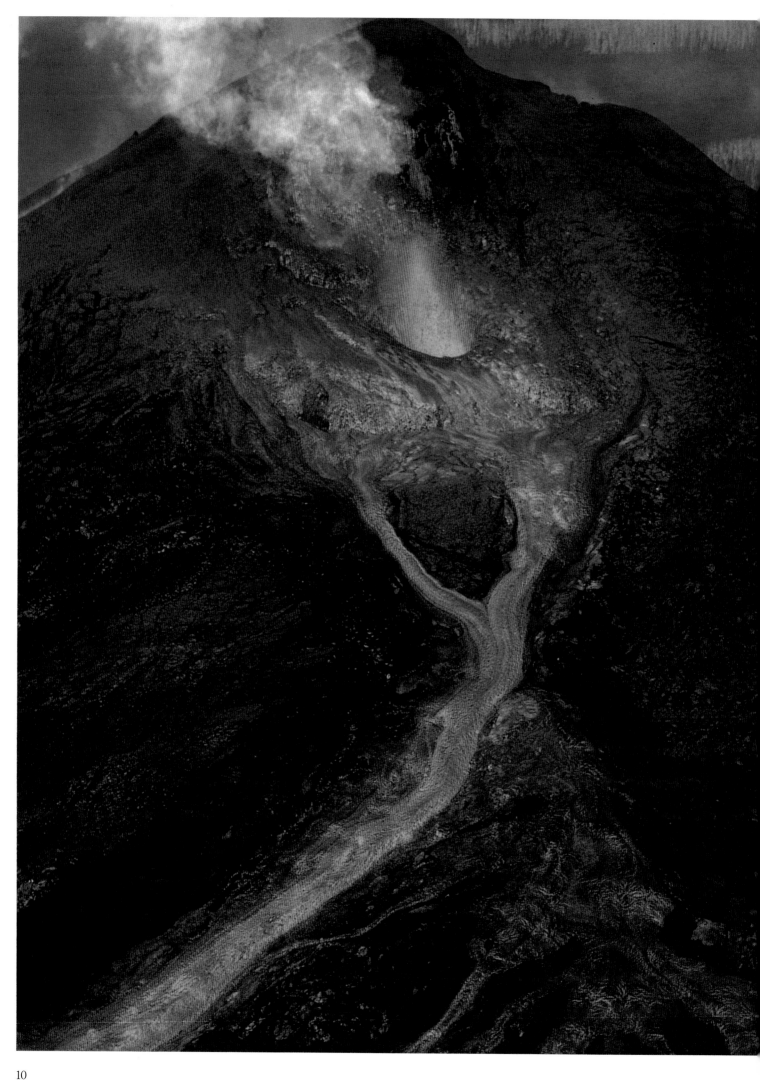

INTRODUCTION

*B*orn of volcanic fires, sculpted in isolation, and matured into an earthly paradise, Hawaii is a land of powerful contrasts, where the natural and the supernatural co-exist.

The islands of Hawaii, with their unique combination of dramatic beauty and remoteness, incite in the beholder a feeling of awe and wonder. Here, molten red lava snakes through lush, fern valleys; freezing snowcapped mountains loom above sun-baked, black sand beaches, and everything appears to be washed with color from a seemingly ever-present rainbow hovering across the horizon.

These haunting contrasts find their beginnings in the fiery birth of the islands. Eons ago, from the deep, dark Neptunian depths of the ocean floor came at first a seismic rumbling. This shuddering grew until a massive explosion of molten lava (known as magma) shot up from the earth's core and began the slow process of building the Hawaiian Islands, layer by layer.

This source of heat and molten lava is referred to as Hawaii's "hot spot." It continued to spew its land-forming contents for the next million years as the earth's floating tectonic plates inched over it. Gradually, the islands of Hawaii were formed — from ancient Kure (now eroded into an atoll, 1,367 miles northwest of Honolulu) to the newest island, the Big Island of Hawaii.

The rounded, shield-type volcanoes emerged above the ocean's surface to eventually produce the eight major islands in the Hawaiian chain that we see today. Kauai was formed nearly six million years ago. Three million years later, as the tectonic plate continued to slide northwestward, the island of Oahu appeared, made up of two more volcanoes: Waianae and Koolau. Then a series of six volcanoes created what is now Molokai, Lanai, Kahoolawe, and Maui over a million years ago. Less than half a million years ago the final visible island in the chain, the Big Island of Hawaii, sprang up from the ocean depths from five volcanoes: Mauna Kea, Mauna Loa, Hualalai, Kohala, and Kilauea.

Only the volcanoes on the Big Island continue to erupt today. Mauna Loa last awoke in 1984 with a 1,500-foot "curtain of fire" and Kilauea, the most active, has been erupting continuously since January 1983.

Mother Nature isn't finished yet.

As the tectonic plate even now continues its journey northwestward, a new volcano is being formed beneath the sea, 13 to 15 miles southwest of the Big Island. Named Loihi, scientists estimate the emerging island is now 3,000 feet beneath the surface and will break through in about 10,000 years.

Each of Hawaii's islands rose above the ocean's waves pristine and virginal. More than 2,000 miles from the closest major landmass, these volcanoes were simply cooled black lava rock, devoid of all vegetation.

Trade winds, a constantly moving sea, and ocean-going sea birds brought seeds and spores from far away that took hold in the new landmass. It was a slow process: one species arrived about every 40,000 years. But once there they thrived, nourished by the rich, volcanic soil, abundant rainfall, and sunshine. Hawaii is now home to some 2,500 plants, evolved from just a few early species. Many have been lost since the islands' discovery by man, but they still represent perhaps the most diversity from the smallest number of progenitors in the world.

The earth's most remote island chain, Hawaii lays claim to several other world records:
- ▲ The wettest spot: On the upper slopes of Mt. Waialeale on Kauai, 451 inches is considered to be average rainfall
- ▲ The highest mountain: Mauna Kea, measured from ocean floor to its permanently snowcapped peak is 32,000 feet
- ▲ The longest waterfall: Water tumbling down the Kahiwa waterfall on Molokai drops 1,750 feet
- ▲ The steepest cliffs: The sheer rock faces on the north shore of Molokai measure 4,000 vertical feet

Left: Kilauea lava flow, Big Island of Hawaii.
Above: Waterfalls at Mount Waialeale Crater, Kauai.

The islands' remoteness has also produced not only plants but birds unique to Hawaii, such as the Koloa duck, the *io* (Hawaiian hawk), and the *pueo* (short-eared Hawaiian owl). Many were flightless as they did not need to fly to find food or escape predators. Of the 66 Hawaiian birds that once existed, 40 percent are now extinct and 45 percent are either endangered or threatened. In fact, Hawaiian birds and plants are considered to be among the most endangered in the world; Hawaiian birds account for more than half of all the birds listed in the "Red Book of Rare and Endangered Species" of the U.S. Bureau of Sport Fisheries and Wildlife. Among the extinct species are flightless rails, thrushes, honey eaters, and honey creepers.

For the most part, Hawaiian birds disappeared for two main reasons: over-hunting by early Polynesian settlers who prized their beautiful feathers, and the introduction of animals to Hawaii that either ate the birds, their eggs, their food, or competed more successfully for the birds' nesting areas.

These animals were brought to Hawaii, either accidentally or purposely, by nearly every group of people immigrating there. Once there, many became wild. Feral animals such as goats and pigs have wreaked havoc on the delicate Hawaiian ecosystem. The only mammals native to Hawaii are the Hawiian bat and the Hawaiian monk seal.

Human discovery of Hawaii came in about the 10th century—comparatively recent in Hawaii's history. The first people to discover the Islands were the the seafaring Polynesians, who, after settling first on the island of Tahiti, continued

east on their voyages of discovery in search of new places to raise their families. Two thousand five hundred miles later, sailing in double-hulled, ocean-going canoes called outriggers, they reached the islands they named "Hawaii."

Nearly 800 years later, in the 18th century, Captain Cook was the first of many European and American explorers and traders who arrived looking for commerce. They were followed a few years later by American missionaries seeking to save the souls of the native people.

As the population and commerce increased, the next wave of immigrants came from Asia and Europe looking for work and, like the first Polynesians, they sought opportunities for a better life. Today, more people than ever flock to the melting pot that is Hawaii. Most are visitors seeking the beauty and indescribable magic of the islands.

People come to Hawaii for many reasons: to enjoy the tropical sunshine, gentle afternoon breezes, soft ocean mists, and to listen to the steady rolling surf; or perhaps to take a leisurely helicopter tour of the islands and behold Hawaii's spectacular scenery from a new perspective.

Some seek the more active life: the satisfying thud of a tennis ball against a racket on a sun-drenched court or the incomparable smell of newly mown grass on a manicured golf course. For others, the opportunity simply to marvel at panoramic views of Hawaii from atop a cliff after an arduous climb or to feel the rippling motion of the wind through their hair as they make the thrilling bike ride down the slopes of 10,000-foot Haleakala is reward enough.

Opposite, top left and right: Native Hawaiians. Opposite, middle left: O'o birds. Opposite, bottom left: I'iwi birds. Top: The great seafaring Polynesians. Middle: Hawaiian birds are considered to be among the most endangered in the world. Bottom: Ohelo berries.

The ocean holds promise for many. They come to skim over its surface on windsurf boards, to plunge under the waves and experience the enchanting underwater world, and to test their luck and skill in battling the deep sea big game fish. There is also the lure of history. The remains of ancient temples dot the landscape and tell the story of an ancient way of life all but vanished from these islands. One can explore Hawaii's maritime past and clamber aboard replicas of old whaling ships, or, on Molokai, stand in reverence at the grave of the dedicated lepers' priest, Father Damien. For many, the sole purpose of the trip is the chance to view the emotionally moving USS Arizona Memorial at Pearl Harbor and consider the fate of American heroes in World War II.

But most of all, people make the trip to Hawaii because of the beauty and promise of an experience quite removed from life on the mainland. Cresting azure waves pummel black and tan-colored beaches; curved palm trees dance in the breeze; a breathtaking sunrise illuminates Haleakala Crater; muted colors paint the sky at sunset; shapely dancers with long, flowing hair perform the traditional Hawaiian hula with gyrating hips; and exotic foods such as juicy, golden pineapples, sweet, buttery macadamia nuts, and roast pig, poi, and other unusual fare appear as part of the popular Hawaiian tradition of the luau. And through it all, the fragrance of tropical flowers—vibrant orchids, heart-shaped anthuriums, and sweet, fragranced plumerias—is intoxicating.

These images are the public face of Hawaii. The face of an American tourist attraction with an exotic accent. But Hawaii has another face, a private, mysterious face that is not easily accessible.

There is a hidden Hawaii, a Hawaii few people see. Deep within the islands' inaccessible, dramatically scenic valleys exist abundant wildlife and the undisturbed remnants of an ancient civilization quite different from our own.

Hindered by topography, only a few hardy people and those with access to a helicopter can scale the several-thousand-foot-high sea cliffs guarding untouched hidden valleys. Here birds hover in the winds, voluptuous trees tower over delicate ferns, and vibrant-hued flowers stand out aganst the multi-shaded greenery. Rushing streams filled with tiny shrimp dart down hillsides, around boulders, and over tiny pebbles. Sunlight pours dazzlingly through shade trees, and amorphous shadows spread over the richly colored earth.

Even fewer people will venture into Hawaii's nearly inaccessible rain forests where mist constantly permeates the air and the vegetation is so thick it appears to have grown into a solid, impenetrable mass.

In these hidden places thunderous waterfalls cascade down the face of sheer cliffs creating a euphonious symphony of water music. Serene, remote mountain lakes lie in perfect tranquility, untouched by Man. The air is filled with the humus smell of a fertile earth.

Left: Maakua Gulch, Oahu.
Above: Waikiki Beach, Oahu.

Hawaii's rare and endangered plants still thrive in these valleys and forests and its endangered birds still sing. The plaintive staccato call of the nene goose carries across windswept grasslands; remnants of a former nesting site of a Hawaiian crow litter the ground; and brief white flashes against the dark night sky betray the flight pattern of the pueo, the short-eared Hawaiian owl.

In such out-of-the-way places evidence of an ancient people that passed this way is all around: petroglyphs (figures carved into rocks), ruined rock walls (the remains of home sites, shrines, and temples), and burial grounds.

These artifacts begin to form a picture of a way of life where people lived in harmony with the land and sea in pie-shaped areas called *ahupuaa,* stretching from the mountain tops down to the ocean. The ancient Hawaiians were governed by chiefs (*alii*) and they respected a strict code of laws called *kapu.* Breaking some of these laws called for the death penalty unless the offender was able to outrun the chief's men to "a Place of Refuge" where he was given sanctuary. Remains of such places still exist.

It was kapu (forbidden) for women to eat pork, bananas, coconuts, and certain types of fish. Wives were never allowed to eat with their husbands. A commoner had to take care to prevent his shadow from falling across the house of a chief. When a chief traveled during the day, everyone who saw him had to prostrate himself on the ground immediately. When he sat down to eat, everyone in his presence had to kneel. The penalty for breaking these kapu could be death.

The ancient Hawaiian religious beliefs were based on the sacred power of nature. In the logical philosophy of today's world, many artifacts and ancient legends remain unexplained and shrouded in mystery.

KAUAI

NIIHAU

OAHU

MOLOKAI

STATE OF HAWAII

LANAI

MAUI

KAHOOLAWE

HAWAII

For example, there is a temple on the north tip of the Big Island called Mookini where royalty fasted, prayed, and occasionally offered human sacrifices to their gods—principally the god of war, Ku. Archeologists have puzzled for years over how the temple was built. The rocks forming the temple have been scientifically verified to originate from a remote valley 10 miles away. Even the ancient legend agrees on this fact. But the legend also claims this huge temple was built in just a single night by a human chain, 10 miles long, lining up and down steep valleys, which passed the stones hand to hand.

In the northeastern corner of Maui, outside the village of Hana, the waters inside a certain cave turn bright red once a year. Scientists have a range of theories, but the Hawaiians point to the legend, which says that the red water is the blood of two lovers who died there.

Probably the most powerful legends center around Pele, the volcano goddess. Still worshipped today, offerings of flowers and ti leaves left by her followers can be seen on the slopes of Kilauea Volcano on the Big Island. Her followers point to the spewing volcanic eruptions as evidence of the existence of their goddess.

People claim to have seen Pele's face in the fountaining lava or in the portentous plumes of white steam rising above the point where the sizzling lava flows into the ocean. Believers in Pele and nonbelievers do agree that there is no denying the unappeasable power in the ability of the molten lava to annihilate everything in its path.

And so the cycle of construction and destruction continues. Violent volcanic eruptions give birth to peaceful islands of beauty and mystery. The Hawaiians have a word that means hello, goodbye, and love: *aloha*. This book is a journey into the land of aloha: the land of dramatic contrasts, new beginnings, violent endings, amid shimmering beauty and love.

Left: City of Refuge, Big Island of Hawaii.
Above: Graceful hula dancer silhouetted at sunset.

Na Pali Coast.

Kauai
& Niihau

Formed by the volcano Mt. Waialeale some 6.5 million years ago, Kauai is not only the oldest island in the main Hawaiian chain, but also, due to its age, the most verdant. Dubbed the Garden Isle, this northernmost island has a place in history as the first island Captain Cook visited in 1778, and the only island The Great Unifier, Kamehameha the Great, did not conquer. Its razor-edged Na Pali Cliffs overlook endless white sand beaches and pounding surf. No less spectacular is Waimea Canyon (named the Grand Canyon of the Pacific by Mark Twain), and the inaccessible jungle forests and numerous cascading waterfalls to be found throughout the island. Nevertheless, Man has succeeded in taming the wild beauty of the island enough to produce sugarcane, pineapple, and taro in the fertile volcanic soil.

Known as "The Forbidden Island" because it is off-limits to outsiders, Niihau is today the only island that retains native Hawaiian language and culture. The Robinson family has owned the island since 1864. Today, the Robinson cattle ranch employs most of the residents.

Niihau is perhaps most celebrated for its beautiful shell lei necklaces, made from tiny white, burgundy, flecked, or brown lustrous shells. The leis are priced as fine jewelry, and regarded as treasures by collectors.

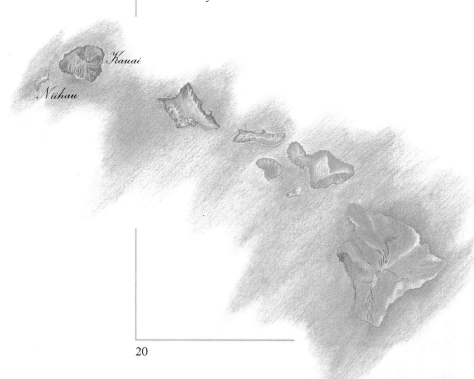

Kauai

Niihau

Hanalei Bay.

The Wailua is Hawaii's only navigable river. It once ran faster and deeper. In those days, sailing ships would sweep in from the ocean and glide up the broad, calm waters. The name Wailua means ghostly, sacred, or twin waters. At Wailua Falls, the river tumbles over an 80-foot cliff in a double torrent. Birds swoop in and out of its mist.

The ancestors of the Hawaiian people, colonizers from Tahiti, first settled on Kauai at Wailua approximately 800 A.D. The great chief Puna made his home beside the river and established the alii or nobility class of settlers. Seven sacred temples were built at intervals along the Wailua, including one of the oldest in Hawaii, Holo Holu Ku Heiau. A huge cave which yawns beside the river was named Fern Grotto as it is so draped in ferns that some grow upside down from the ceiling.

Left: Wailua Falls. Above: Black-necked stilt. Below: Fern Grotto on the Wailua River.

Kauai is lush and fertile, the oldest major island in the chain. The first sugar plantation in the islands was here and the first sugar mill was built at Koloa in 1836. Sugar continues to sweeten Kauai's life. Most of the people still live in small plantation towns with populations under 4,000.

At Hanalei, glistening wet fields of taro are grown and harvested as they have been for centuries. The spinach-like leaves are steamed as a favorite vegetable while the roots are pounded for notorious poi, the traditional Hawaiian dietary staple.

Botanical gardens, banana and papaya plantations, and the largest guava orchard in the world thrive on this rural outpost island.

Left: Hanalei Valley taro farm. Left, inset: Taro crop.
Below: McBryde Sugar Mill.

Called the Grand Canyon of the Pacific, Waimea stretches to the horizon in tawny shades of ochre and umber. Wild and untamed, parts of it unexplored, it is home to nimble mountain goats and to rare Hawaiian birds that swoop in the vagrant wind currents of the canyon. The stratified lava that formed Kauai lays exposed to the sunshine and shadows. Through millennia, heavy rainfall carved this raw gorge more than 14 miles long and 2,857 feet deep, so precipitous in places that the valley floor never sees a sunrise or a sunset, and lies in a perpetual twilight. Flowing through the heart of the canyon is the Waimea River, carrying away more of Kauai's earth as it reveals more of the island's secret past.

Above: A vast expanse of Waimea Canyon. Right: An incredible view from Waimea Canyon lookout.

Scented with pine and dressed in forests of native koa and wild plum, Kokee State Park overlooks the wide green Kalalau Valley at the head of the Na Pali Coast. The 4,345-acre preserve is laced with 45 miles of hiking trails. Uninhabited now, archaeological evidence indicates that Kalalau was first settled by Polynesians from the Marquesas Islands before the Tahitians reached Hawaii. Jack London wrote one of his most famous stories, *Koolau the Leper*, about a Hawaiian cowboy from Waimea who contracted the dread disease and led a small band of victims into Kalalau where they held out against the authorities who wanted to imprison them on Molokai. Kalalau is often called the Valley of the Lost Tribe.

Above: Kokee State Park. Right: Colorful blossoms of plumeria. Far right: Sunset at Kokee State Park beach.

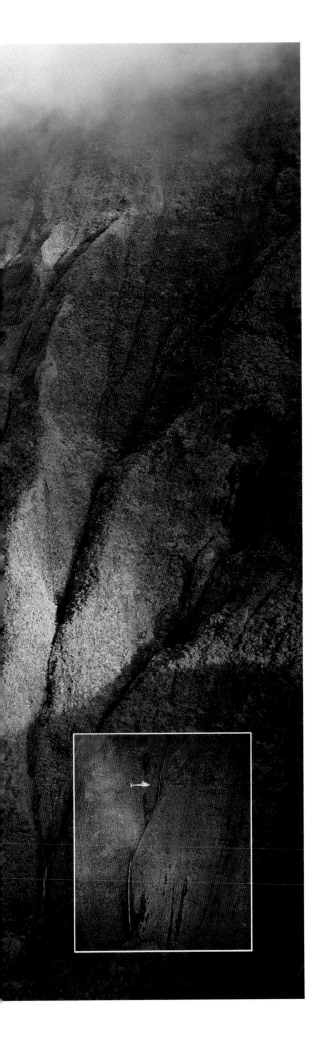

All 533 square miles of Kauai were built by one massive volcano, Mount Waialeale, eight million years old. The massive eastern rim of the caldera is its venerable relic. Weeping in streams of waterfalls, the 3,000-foot cliffs are lettuce green and bowl-shaped. They are shrouded in mist with shafts of sunlight piercing the sheltering clouds. Translated, the mountain's name is "overflowing waters." Waialeale's Alakai Swamp is the wettest place on Earth, averaging 460 inches of rain annually. In one especially wet year, 624 inches fell. Legend has it that the row of trees appearing in the photograph below were planted to serve as a guide for people walking through the misty swamp.

Left: Mount Waialeale Crater. Left, inset: A helicopter ride provides a unique view of the crater. Below: Alakai Swamp.

West of Haena Point.

Mamalahoa Mountain.

At the headland known as Ka Lae o Kilauea, a brilliant beam reaches out into the blackness of the Pacific from Kilauea Lighthouse, almost a century old. The light was originally built at the request of Prince Jonah Kuhio Kalanianole, Kauai's royal Territorial Delegate to the U.S. Congress. The site is now listed on the National Register of Historic Places, and is a wildlife refuge. It is possible to see, in season, turtles, dolphins, monk seals, and humpback whales, along with flocks of seabirds.

Above and right: Two views of Kilauea Lighthouse.

Called The Forbidden Island, 73-square-mile Niihau, lying just 17 miles across the Kaulakahi Channel from Kauai, is off-limits to all but the 300 Hawaiian people who live there and who continue to speak Hawaiian as their primary language. Originally purchased in 1864 from King Kamehameha V by a Scottish widow, Niihau is still privately owned by her descendants, the Robinson family of Kauai, who run a cattle ranch on the island. The island has but one village, Puuwai, and the largest lake, Halalii, in the state.

Women of Niihau are known for their artistry in creating the famed Niihau shell leis, prized by collectors. The tiny shells, found only on these beaches, are fashioned into intricate necklaces and bracelets of complicated design.

Left: The Forbidden Island of Niihau. Top: Niihau shells that will be fashioned into leis. Above, inset: Lehua Island, an extinct volcano crater, is located northwest of Niihau.

A rare view of Honolulu from the Nu'uanu Pali.

Oahu

*T*he third largest island, Oahu houses 80 percent of Hawaii's population and is aptly known as "The Gathering Place." Oahu is home to the state capital and is also the center of its finance and industry. There is something for everyone on this island, from the bright lights and non-stop bustle of downtown Waikiki to the slower-paced, relaxed country life of the rural windward (east) side. Renowned for the landmark Diamond Head Crater (named by sailors who thought crystals they found on the crater were diamonds), Oahu also features many other attractions: the somber but eloquent USS Arizona Memorial at Pearl Harbor, excellent surfing on the North Shore, snorkeling amid a rainbow multitude of fish in Hanauma Bay, lively marine shows at Sea Life Park, and the swaying dancers of the Kodak hula show, among others.

Oahu

Diamond Head.

At a place called Haiku, on the windward side of Oahu, beneath the emerald spires of the Koolaus, the Byodo-In sits like a pearl of great price. Crowning Hawaiian Memorial Park, the vermillion temple is a replica of the famous Byodo-In Temple of Equality in Kyoto, Japan. The great golden Buddha of the Western Paradise presides over the main pavilion. In the garden are quiet corners for meditation. Peacocks stretch their showy plumes. In the waters of a two-acre lake, hundreds of golden koi, the prized carp, swim about flashing their mottled, glimmering beauty.

Top: Byodo-In Temple. Above: An enchanting lily pond. Right: Golden koi, the prized carp.

Professional penguins, leaping whales, performing porpoise, and sea lions with roaring appetites are just a few of the residents of Sea Life Park, an aquatic wonderland located at Makapuu Point, where the dry sunny southeastern coast of Oahu meets the lush windward side.

Nearby, at the 40-acre Polynesian Cultural Center, the arts, music, and dance of seven Pacific Island groups are shared with the world. Hawaii, Tahiti, Samoa, Fiji, Tonga, the Marquesas, and Aotearoa (Maori New Zealand) each has its own village beside lagoons and among palm trees.

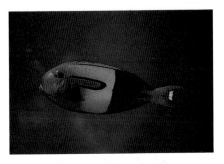

Left: Polynesian Cultural Center. Left, inset: Native dancers perform for visitors. Top: Sea Life Park. Middle left: Sea birds are a common sight at Makapuu Beach. Middle right and bottom left: Just several of the many types of fish that can be seen in Sea Life Park's oceanarium. Bottom right: False killer whale.

True to its name, Sunset Beach is the favorite spot to view the spectacular sunsets that light up the evening sky. The beach's natural beauty is highlighted by the golden sand and ironwood trees which frame the turquoise-hued tropical water. Although the surf is calm in summer, winter storms churn up giant 30-foot waves that make Sunset Beach the premier surfing beach on Oahu's North Shore.

Left: Sunset Beach. Above: Surfing Sunset Beach.

Circular Hanauma Bay is a volcanic crater whose walls were breached by the ocean eons ago, forming a protected cove. A complex reef system developed, supporting thousands of fish which came to dwell in the sheltered waters. The bay was once the favorite fishing grounds of King Kamehameha V, and for the shore-casters and throw-net fishermen from all over Oahu.

In 1967, Hanauma Bay became an underwater park and marine life sanctuary, making it unlawful to remove or kill any shell or fish. It is estimated that 10,000 people a day visit Hanauma Bay.

Above: Hanauma Bay. Right: Colorful varieties of sea life abound in this marine life sanctuary.

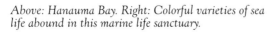

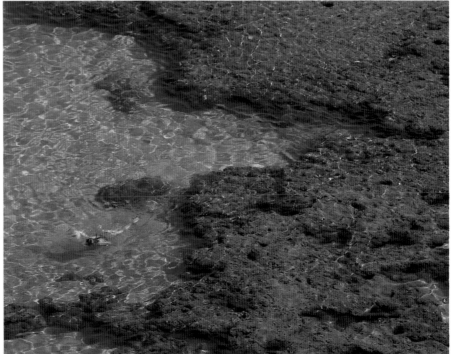

Famous Waikiki Beach is not just one beach, but a lei of beaches stretching for two sandy miles from Diamond Head at one end to the Duke Kahanamoku Lagoon at the other. Queen Liliuo-kalani had a home called Hamohamo right in the heart of Waikiki, and Princess Kaiulani once sat beneath the Moana Hotel's enormous banyan tree and listened while her friend Robert Louis Stevenson read her stories he had written.

The Moana, built in 1901, was the first hotel in Waikiki, followed by the Pink Palace of the Pacific, the Royal Hawaiian Hotel. Movie stars and beach boys, presidents and canoe paddlers, kings and commoners all mixed happily in this former royal playground.

Waikiki today is still Hawaii's premier resort, lavished with money and attention and still drawing the rich, the royal, and sun-seekers of every stature.

Left: Waikiki Beach, Hawaii's premier vacation spot.
Above: Honolulu and Ala Moana Park.

Above: Makapuu Point Lighthouse. Right: Pali Range in the Oahu back country.

The island of Oahu was formed by the activity of two giant, dome-like shield volcanoes, Waianae and Koolau. The lava flows met, creating a central plateau called Leilehua. Time, wind, and rain sculpted the younger volcano, Koolau, into what appears to be a mountain range running along the spine of the island. Spectacular Nu'uanu Pali on the windward side is a natural cliff rampart which affords one of the most beautiful views in the world.

It was at a pass in these mountains that the invading army of Kamehameha the Great, soon to be the first king of the Hawaiian Islands, drove the retreating army of Oahu over the thousand-foot precipices to their deaths. The famous battle is depicted here in a painting by noted Hawaiian artist and historian Herb Kawainui Kane.

Left: Puu Kanehoalani mountain range. Above: King Kamehameha I. Below: The Battle of Nu'uanu Pali, 1795.

December 7, 1941, was just another peaceful, sunny Sunday morning in Hawaii when suddenly a fleet of Japanese dive bombers swooped over Oahu, bombing and strafing as they swept through the mountain passes and descended on Pearl Harbor. In a two-hour bombardment, the toll was eight battleships destroyed, along with 10 other combat ships, 188 aircraft in ruins, and a shattering 2,403 American lives lost. Despite crippling American naval forces, the surprise attack triggered this country's entry into World War II.

The gleaming white Arizona Memorial in Pearl Harbor shelters the sunken hulk of the *USS Arizona* battleship that sank with 1,100 men aboard. In a concert held on March 25, 1961, Elvis Presley raised a large portion of the funds that built the memorial. Today it is Hawaii's most visited site.

Left: Pearl Harbor. Far left, inset: USS Arizona Memorial. Left, inset: Wreckage of a United States World War II fighter plane on an inaccessible ridge seen only by helicopter. Above: Pearl Harbor shipwreck.

Tall kings, robed in red and gold feathers, and crowned with Roman-like helmets, once ruled an island nation first united by King Kamehameha I. During their reign the greatest flowering of Polynesian culture took place. But in 1819, after the death of Kamehameha, the Hawaiians spurned their ancient religion, tore down their temples, and burned the tiki god images.

With the arrival of the first American missionaries in 1820, the Hawaiian language was given a written form. Literacy was achieved in one generation. The himeni, hymns, brought a new dimension to Hawaii's traditional chants and hula.

Hawaiian royalty, now garbed in satin and jewels, was received in the courts of Europe. King David Kalakaua built Iolani Palace on the site of a more modest royal palace. It was in the Blue Room of the palace that Queen Liliuokalani was deposed by a revolutionary contingent of American settlers, paving the way for the eventual annexation by the United States, and statehood in 1959.

Left: Makapuu Point. Above: Iolani Palace, the only royal palace in the United States.

Church at Kalawao.

Molokai

*T*hirty-seven-by-ten-mile Molokai, formed by three volcanoes, has the highest cliffs and waterfalls in the world. But this spectacular island was also witness to ancient Polynesian rituals and much later, one of the saddest examples of man's inhumanity to man.

In the 19th century, the island's Kalaupapa Peninsula came to be used as an isolated confinement for hundreds of leprosy sufferers, who were left to die there without hope of cure. Largely due to the heroic efforts of Father Damien, a Belgian priest, who fought hard on their behalf, they were not completely forgotten. Eventually, curative drugs were found that all but wiped out the disease. Today, the island once known as the "The Lonely" or "Forgotten" Isle has been renamed the "Friendly" Isle because of its high concentration of native Hawaiians.

Molokai

Leina o Papio Point.

The highest sea cliffs in the world tower along the windward northern shore of Molokai. The colossal 2,000-foot rampart is breached by deep valleys, assaulted by wind and rain, and adorned with shimmering waterfalls. One of these, Kahiwa Falls, at 1,750 feet is the highest cascade in the state. It plunges in tiers into the foaming waters of the Pailolo Channel.

In ancient times, Molokai maintained its independence not by the might of its warriors, for the island was too small and sparsely inhabited to field an army, but by the reputation of its kahunas or priests, known for their remarkable powers of sorcery. The traditional name of the island is Molokai Pule O'o, Molokai of the Powerful Prayer.

Left: Misty view of Leina o Papio Point.
Above: Kahiwa Falls.

The Hawaiians were not only skilled fishermen, they were also the first to pioneer the science of aquaculture to assure themselves of a steady supply of fish, regardless of the weather or season. They constructed an amazing network of fishponds with elaborate gatekeeping and a technology based on a sophisticated knowledge of environmental factors. The fishponds ringed the shores of all islands. In these ponds the ancient farmers of the sea developed the ability to grow and harvest fish. Without a written language, many of the techniques have been lost. Scientists only recently have rediscovered the old wisdom.

Left: Ali'i Fishponds. Top: Kamalo Fishponds. Above, left: Spearfisher, circa 1890.

The first case of leprosy appeared in Hawaii in 1840. In two decades, it cut such a swath through the defenseless population that King Kamehameha V was forced to exile the infected. Because of its topography and isolation, Makanalua Peninsula on Molokai's north shore, now popularly called Kalaupapa, was chosen. It became a lawless community of sick and desperate people whose only governor was Death. Into this milieu Father Damien, a Belgian priest, brought comfort, built shelters, and introduced order. He badgered the authorities for more food and supplies and built a church, a hospital, an orphanage, cottages, and a water system. He started farms, visited the sick, dressed wounds, and buried the dead (6,000 of them during his time). Finally he, too, succumbed to the dreaded disease. Today, he is a candidate for sainthood in the Roman Catholic Church.

Left: Kalaupapa Peninsula. Far left, inset: Lae O Kahiu Lighthouse. Left, inset: Kalaupapa Landing. Note the woman in the foreground with her arms bandaged due to leprosy. Above: Father Damien's grave. Below: St. Philomena, Father Damien's church.

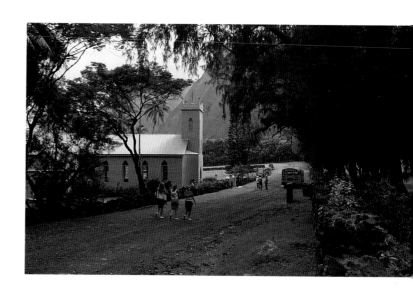

W ild and lonely stretches of beach with
wondrous-sounding names like Pukoo,
Moomomi, Kawakiu, and Pohakumauliuli are part
of Molokai's enchantment. There are no footprints
in the sand. These beaches are undisturbed, pristine,
and far from the crowds. Sunsets come with fiery
skies, as day gives way to night. Across the channel,
only 12 jet minutes away, the lights of Honolulu
sparkle like stars fallen to the earth.

Above and right:
Stretches of deserted beach.

Cape Halawa is the barrier of Halawa Valley, site of an ancient civilization. Ruined temples and villages lie choked by jungle. The valley, which runs four miles deep, is the only one acessible by car. At its head are two towering waterfalls. The longest, Moaula Falls, is the legendary home of a giant dragon. Hikers who wish to swim in its pool would be wise to check up on the dragon first by tossing a ti leaf into the water. If the leaf floats, the dragon is away and it's safe to swim. If it sinks—beware.

Above: Moaula Falls, located at the head of Halawa Valley. Right: Inlet near the mouth of Halawa Valley.

Above: Coast near Halawa Valley. Top right: Picturesque church in Halawa Valley. Bottom right: A mule ride up Molokai's winding, hillside paths.

Molokai deserves to be better known, for it offers very diverse attractions. One of the most popular is the Molokai Mule Ride. Astride well-trained animals, visitors tackle the switchback trail that leads down to Kalaupapa. The former exile colony is now a National Historical Park, and one of the most beautiful spots in Hawaii.

Molokai's wilderness areas shelter a variety of wildlife including wild turkeys and other game birds, axis deer, boar, and goats. The Molokai Ranch, in an effort to control the brush encroaching on pastureland, imported animals from Africa to eat the shrubs. Happily at home on the range, in terrain similar to their native land, the animals have thrived and the ranch now runs camera safaris into the preserve.

Sunset at Kaanapali Beach.

Maui
& Lanai

O ver a million years ago, the lava erupting from the 10,000-foot Haleakala volcano spewed down the sides of the mammoth mountain and bridged the gap to the older West Maui volcano, thereby creating an isthmus that became the island of Maui.

Maui is topographically diverse and therefore possesses several micro-climates. Haleakala National Park alone encompasses the whole range, from the stark, cold lunarscape of its summit crater to the warm, lush, tropical Kipahulu rain forest and shoreline washed by azure waves and waving palm trees at the southeastern end of the park. Because of this range, Haleakala National Park was protected in 1980 as an International Biosphere Reserve by UNESCO. It is home to the rare silversword plant (which blooms once every 100 years, then dies) and the endangered nene (Hawaiian goose).

Appropriately named Pineapple Island, Lanai has been a pineapple plantation (owned by Dole Pineapple) since the 1920s. Over the years, most of the 2,000 residents of Lanai have worked for the 16,000-acre pineapple plantation (one of the world's largest). However, times are changing on this humpback-shaped, 140-square-mile island. Hotels and resorts are being built that will allow tourists to explore the miles of high-country jeep trails, deserted, hidden beaches, and broad, coral-reef flats.

Lanai

Maui

Haleakala National Park.

Top: Cane and pineapple fields in North Maui. Above left: Children displaying Maui onions. Above middle: Macadamia cluster. Above right: View of Molokai from Maui. Right, inset: Pineapple harvesting.

Maui comes in a hundred hues of green, stitched together in a crazy quilt pattern of pineapple fields, sugar plantations, and the newer crop of macadamia nuts. Small farms growing vegetables, fruits, herbs, and flowers add to the texture. A year-round growing season, fertile volcanic soil, and efficient agricultural techniques give most Hawaiian crops the highest yield per acre in the world. Besides pineapple, other major fruits grown in the Islands are banana, passion fruit, papaya, orange, tangerine, avocado, and guava.

Lahaina was once the capital of the Hawaiian kingdom. The town gained its notoriety after the arrival of the first whaling ship in 1819, the *Balena,* out of New Bedford, Massachusetts. By 1846, the height of the Yankee whaling era in the Pacific, the harbor was a forest of masts with 429 whaling ships spilling as many as 1,500 party-hungry sailors ashore at a time. Their clashes with the New England missionaries who had settled in the town are legendary. The old weathered buildings along Front Street, survivors of those lusty days, were declared a National Historic Preservation District in 1962. Lahaina continues to look like a little piece of New England tucked among the palms.

Above: Lahaina. Below: This figure of a sailor is reminiscent of Lahaina's whaling era. Right: Lahaina Harbor.

In the warm waters of the Hawaiian Islands, the great humpback whales gather every winter. They migrate from their Arctic feeding grounds to mate and give birth. On the very brink of extinction, they sing their haunting whale song. It is speculated that only the male sings, as part of his courting ritual. Humpbacks are baleen whales, which have no teeth. They feed on very small prey, their main food being krill, an eight-inch long crustacean. Amazingly, on such a diet they can grow to a length of 62 feet and a weight of 53 tons. Although the humpbacks are found in all Hawaiian waters between November and June, the calm waters between Maui, Molokai, and Lanai seem to be their favorite haven. The area has been declared a cetacean sanctuary. Other species of whales found in the waters around Hawaii are the sperm whale, false killer whale, and pilot whale.

Left: Great humpback whales.
Above: Humpback whale breaching.

Optimistically called the Hana Highway, the road that leads to remote Hana town is a twisted skein that unravels along a jagged lava coast, beside towering waterfalls, beneath a canopy of rainforest. It spans 54 bridges within 56 miles and is, in many areas, reduced to one lane. It is among the worst roads in the state, and Hana residents like it that way. It keeps the traffic down and enables them to enjoy a lifestyle that is beautifully out of step with 20th-century Hawaii.

Far left: Seven Sacred Pools area. Top: Hana.
Left: Sunrise along Hana Highway.

Dominant 10,023-foot Haleakala Volcano built the entire eastern end of Maui. It was here that the demigod Maui ensnared La, the sun, in his magical lariat and made her travel more slowly across the Hawaiian sky, giving people more time to work and to enjoy themselves. The name Haleakala means House of the Sun.

Haleakala became a national park in 1961. It is home of the endangered nene goose and to the beautiful silversword plant that grows no place else on the planet. People journey to the summit to watch the sunrise at dawn, and hike and ride horseback through the crater. The latest craze is riding a bicycle down the volcano slopes.

Top: Haleakala Crater. Middle: Nenes. Bottom left: Science City. Bottom and far right: Dramatic views of Haleakala Crater.

Above: Haleakala Crater. Top right: South side of Haleakala. Middle, inset: Rare silversword plant. Bottom right: Haleakala Crater.

Few places in Hawaii are more sacred than Iao Valley. Into its deep green folds, the ancient Hawaiians carried their departed alii, or nobility, and laid their bones in secret places. The peace of the valley was interrupted by one of the bloodiest battles in Hawaiian history, when the invading forces of Kamehameha drove the army of Maui's King Kalanikupule into Iao. The roar of cannons reverberated in the valley, felling so many warriors that the Wailuku River waters ran red with blood. So many bodies choked the streams that the battle was called Kepaniwai, meaning "the damming of the waters."

Far left and top: Iao Valley. Above left: Plumeria.

Older than Haleakala, the range called the West Maui Mountains is actually a single shield volcano modified by the elements into a grand sculpture of magnificent proportions. Named Mauna Kahala-wai, it is still largely unexplored. The walls of its valleys weep with waterfalls and at its feet are splendid, isolated beaches. At Iao, the rocks have been naturally sculpted to resemble the craggy profile of President John F. Kennedy. Atop the peaks of the ancient mountain is a natural likeness of a chieftess of ancient times, Lihau. Her body, chiseled by wind and rain, rests between Olowalu and Ukumehame, and her hair trails down to Olowalu. Lahaina lies at the base of these rainbow-haunted hills.

Left and below: West Maui Mountains.
Right: Weeping Wall, West Maui Mountains.

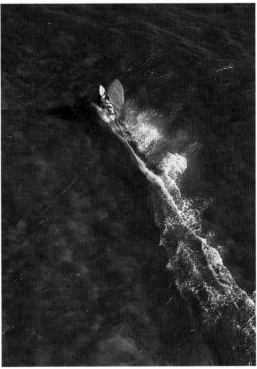

Maui has not one, but two gold coasts: the sunny strip running from Kaanapali to Kapalua, and the breeze-swept fun coast of Kihei, Wailea, and Makena. The windsurfing mecca of the world is Hookipa, and some of the best dive sites in the islands are in the crystal waters of Maui's coral reefs. The island is surrounded by a lei of sandy beaches, from which fleets of outrigger canoes and catamarans set sail daily. Maui just can't live down its reputation as a port of pleasure.

Left: Hookipa Beach. Top: Windsurfing off Maui.
Bottom: Windsurfing Papa'Ula Point.

The remote island of Lanai, sixth largest in the Hawaian chain, was once a part of Maui. In ancient times it was thought to be inhabited by cannibal demons, and it was shunned long after the other islands had been settled. The evil spirits were eventually vanquished by the son of a Maui chieftan and Hawaiians cautiously settled along the shores.

In 1922, the entire island was bought by James Drummond Dole for $1.1 million. He started what is now the world's largest pineapple plantation, shipping 20 million pineapples a month.

The island is about to enter the tourism arena with the debut of two resort hotels, one in the lofty heights of Lanai City and the other along the strip of sand at Hulopoe Beach.

Above and far right: Lanai coast.
Right: Shipwreck Beach.

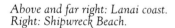

Molokini.

Kilauea lava flow meets the sea.

Hawaii

The youngest and largest of the islands, fiery Hawaii, known simply as the Big Island, contains every type of geographical climate on Earth, except true arctic or desert conditions. Hawaii is made up of five volcanoes, all in different stages of activity. Two are over 13,000 feet and have year-round snowcaps, frigid temperatures, and howling winds. The most active is Kilauea, which is constantly erupting, at once burying the surrounding land and adding new mass to the island's coastline.

Lush tropical rain forest, rolling pastoral cattle ranches, and white, black, and green sand beaches all occupy the same island. Sugarcane, extensive coffee plantations, macadamia nut trees, orchids, and now golf courses and resorts announce that the Big Island has rich and prized resources for both visitors and residents alike.

Hawaii

Laupahoehoe Point Park.

More than twice the size of all the other islands combined, Hawaii is dominated by the tallest mountain in the world, Mauna Kea, "the white mountain." The enormous volcano, which last erupted about 11,000 years ago, rises 13,796 feet above the sea and descends another 19,680 feet to the ocean floor.

Poliahu, goddess of the snows, and ancient enemy of Pele, goddess of fire, is said to dwell in the frosty heights of Mauna Kea. Poliahu is the only one who has ever vanquished the tempestuous Pele, cooling her lava rivers and driving her from Mauna Kea. Pele still inhabits Mauna Loa, "the long mountain," which at 13,677 feet approaches Mauna Kea in height.

Top: View of Mauna Loa from Mauna Kea. Above: Life springs anew from volcanic rock. Right: Cinder cones on Mauna Kea.

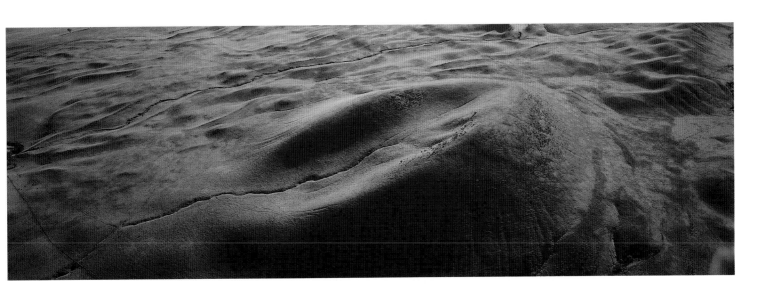

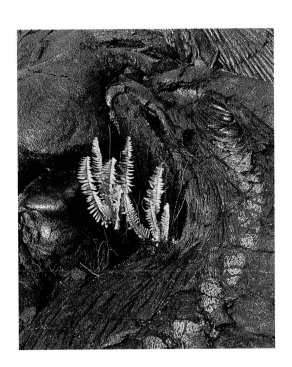

In the depths of the Pacific Ocean, 25 million years ago, far from any landmass, the islands of Hawaii were born in fire. Submarine volcanoes spewed forth molten lava, building first one island and then another as the tectonic land plate inched northwestward over the hot spot in the Pacific Ring of Fire. The process continues to this day. The Big Island's Hawaii Volcanoes National Park encompasses Kilauea, the world's most active volcano, erupting continuously since 1983. Rivers of lava stream toward the sea, burying subdivisions and forests. In the midst of destruction, new life asserts itself in the bright green, delicate ferns that spring from the tortured landscape.

Left, inset: Mauna Loa eruption. Top: Pu'u Oo'o volcano vent. Above: Fern at Hawaii Volcanoes National Park.

Lava pond.

Above: Advancing lava flow of the 1990 Kilauea eruption. Right: The volcano's interface with man; dramatic scenes of Kilauea's past eruptions.

Mauna Kea summit

*Above: Waipio Valley. Top right: Waimanu Valley
coastal area. Bottom right: Jungle near Wailua Falls.*

The Valley of Kings, Waipio, is a broad, verdant notch in the Hamakua Coast. Here the child Kamehameha learned the ways of war and nobility and grew to manhood, hidden from enemies intent on thwarting the prophecy that he would rule the islands and be a killer of chiefs.

In prehistoric times, Waipio supported thousands of farmers who raised taro beside the river, and caught fish there. The twin falls of Hiilawe water the valley, while turquoise surf laps the black sand beach.

Since World War II, two tsunamis (tidal waves) have flooded the valley. A few tenacious taro farmers have returned to till the fertile soil and live in the serenity of this hidden place.

In the bleak desert of Kawaihae, Kamehameha built Puukohola Heiau to honor his war god Kukailimoku before setting out on his campaign to unite all the Hawaiian islands.

The chiefs of Maui, Molokai, and Oahu sent an armada of war canoes to the Big Island to prevent the construction of the heiau, but were defeated. Kamehameha's rival, Keoua, tried to reach Puukohola via Pele's territory of Halemaumau, but his men were killed by the volcano's eruption across their path before they were able to reach their destination. The soldiers' footprints remain in the lava to this day. Puukohola Heiau is a National Historic Site.

Left: Puukohola Heiau National Site.
Left, inset: Petroglyphs at Waikoloa.
Above: Kamehameha and his men.

The eerie beauty of this black sand beach is revealed

In time of war, women, children, and the sick sought shelter within the walls of sanctuaries. Transgressors of the law fled to places of refuge (puuhonua) for atonement, forgiveness, and a new start. There was at least one sanctuary (often called City of Refuge) on each island, often in each district.

Puuhonua o Honaunau, now a National Historic Park, is the most impressive and the best preserved of these sanctuaries. Built around 1550, the 12-acre temple complex is surrounded by a great stone wall, held together by friction, without mortar.

After Kamehameha I, the whole system of religious law (kapu) toppled. Only the Hale o Keawe temple at Puuhonua o Honaunau and the Hale o Lono temple in Waipio Valley remain standing.

Left: Kiilae Bay, City of Refuge. Top: Puuhonua o Honaunau. Above left: Idol at Puuhonua o Honaunau.

Waterfalls abound on the wet, fertile Hilo side of the island. They cascade down the slopes of the Hamakua Coast, plunging into pools on black sand beaches. Elegant Akaka Falls tumbles 420 feet over a sheer cliff into a pool lined with ferns and fragrant ginger. Jungle trails are lined with bamboo, orchids, and giant tree ferns, while blazing red torch ginger and brilliant African tulip trees frame Nanue Falls. Where the Wailuku river plunges into Rainbow Falls, a definite prismatic halo appears at its base in the early morning and the late afternoon. The goddess of the rainbows, Laie-i-kawai dwells in the uplands.

Opposite: Wailua Falls. Opposite, inset: Orchid flower. Top: Waimanu Valley waterfalls. Left: Rainbow Falls.

*E*xperience another Hawaii—
imagine seeing Hawaii as you've
never seen it before. Imagine
a birds-eye view of weathered,
volcanic peaks, towering waterfalls, and swirling clouds. See an
inspiring panorama of precipitous
coastlines, forgotten beaches, and
other-worldly wildlife, punctu-
ated by the timeless ruins of a
past civilization as you approach
in your own private helicopter.
**Experience the Hidden Side of
Hawaii—on a Papillon flight.**

Sightseeing by
helicopter over
Grand Canyon
National Park.

Papillon Hawaii
Helicopters

Since 1975, *Papillon Hawaii Helicopters* every
year provides tens of thousands of Hawaii visitors
with state-of-the-art aerial tours. Papillon offers the
convenience of heliport passenger sites on Oahu,
Kauai, Maui, and Hawaii. These modern helicopters
are specially outfitted for the quietest, most com-
fortable ride. *Papillon* uses only the most highly-
trained, experienced pilots. During each trip, factual
in-flight narration and memorable stereophonic
music heighten visitors' experiences of their tour.
An informative pre- or post-flight audio-visual
presentation, "Hidden Hawaii" brings alive the
sights, sounds, and history of the islands and shows
passengers what they cannot experience on their
flight—a return to the time when the first Polynesian
adventurers discovered Hawaii. *Papillon* offers an
array of tours of all the islands; there is something to
suit every interest. For anyone who has ever dreamed
of seeing the hidden beauty of Hawaii from the lap
of the gods, *Papillon* is the Number One choice.

Moaula Falls,
Molokai.
Explore Hawaii's
tallest sea cliffs,
longest waterfall,
and lushest rain-
forest valleys.

In the Beginning—
The Grand Canyon

From its humble beginnings in 1965, *Grand
Canyon Helicopters*, the forerunner of *Papillon
Airways*, was formed to expose the hidden secrets of
the Grand Canyon of Arizona. Millions of people
have now seen the Grand Canyon from the perspec-
tive of an eagle. *Papillon Airways* today operates
Papillon Grand Canyon Helicopters and *Papillon
Hawaiian Helicopters*.

After 25 years of continuous service, *Papillon
Airways* is proud to be able to say that it has logged
more passenger miles than any other passenger
helicopter operation in the world.

More than 25 years ago when *Papillon Helicopter
Airways* was founded, the helicopter itself was in its
infancy. The biggest concern then was to develop
dependablity into the equipment and find equipment
capable of performing the mission. Just as the helicopter has evolved into a reliable piece of modern
machinery, *Papillon* has evolved within the industry it created. For this entire quarter of a century,
Papillon Airways has been under the same ownership
and management. We are, therefore, able today to
provide our customers with the best scenic tours
ever, in the finest equipment available.

If you have taken a tour with *Papillon Airways*,
you will understand the accolades our passengers
give to the experience. If you have not taken a flight,
we hope someday you will be able to. *Papillon's*
scenic flights create a unique and rare harmony
between nature and modern man.

Come fly with us
again and again.
We love to be
your host.